For Jasper
—L. B.

To my remarkable partner and mutualist family
—R. M.

NATURE'S REMARKABLE PARTNERS

WILD POEMS FOR TWO VOICES

Written by
LESLIE BULION

Illustrated by
ROBERT MEGANCK

Margaret Quinlin Books
PEACHTREE
ATLANTA

Contents

Meet the Mutualists!..8

Please Play with the Poems!...10

Fringed Ornamental Tarantula & Pug-Snout Frog.......................12

Isopods & Red Seaweed..14

Lichen...16

Mountain Treeshrew & Pitcher Plant..18

Carrion Beetle & Mites..20

Ocean Sunfish & Laysan Albatross..22

Egg-Loving Algae & Spotted Salamander Egg.............................24

Leafcutter Ants & Fungi..26

Alligator & Long-Legged Wading Bird...28

Boxer Crab & Anemones...30

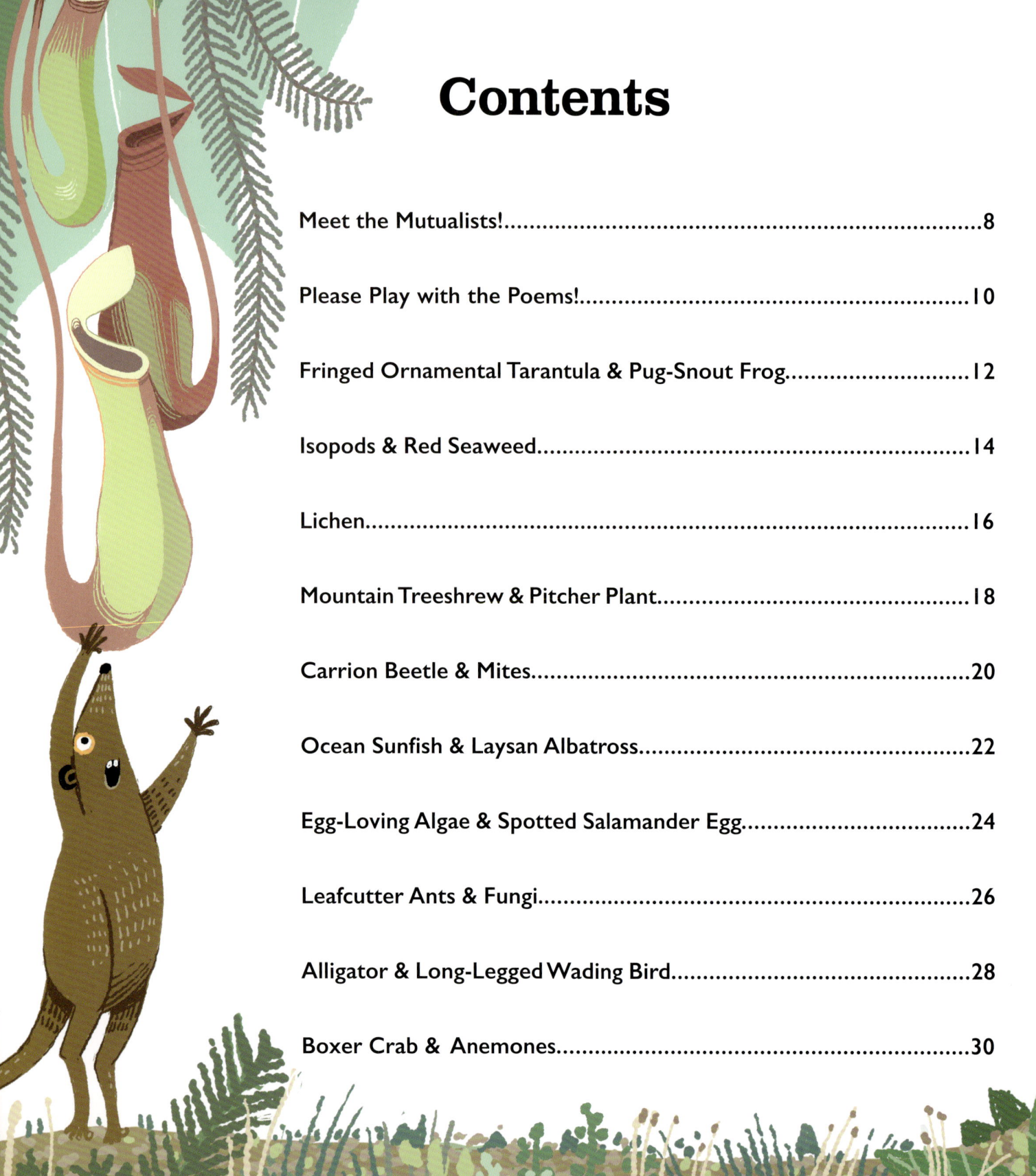

Hawaiian Bobtail Squid & Light Organ Bacteria.................................32

Pistol Shrimp & Goby Fish.................................34

Marsh Frog & Water Buffalo.................................36

Feathered Dinosaur & Beetle Larvae.................................38

Human Being & Gut Bacteria.................................40

Ecosystem Earth!.................................42

Back Matter

    Glossary.................................44

    Remarkable Partners Species List.................................46

    More About Poems for Two Voices.................................47

    Poetry Notes.................................48

    Nature's Wild Relationships.................................50

    Symbiosis and Mutualism: A Bibliography.................................52

    Acknowledgments.................................52

Meet the Mutualists!

Across all Earth habitats, in every nook,
each mountain, each ocean, each burbling brook,
surprising relationships thrive—take a look!
Come see Earth's remarkable partners!

Lots of Earth's life forms live better together—
whether an ant farms its fungi, or whether
an ancient grub gnaws a shed dinosaur feather,
Earth's filled with remarkable partners!

A shrimp shares its burrow and helps a fish hide.
A beetle takes hitchhiker mites for a ride.
Our own gut bacteria tuck in, *inside* . . .
Come see these remarkable partners!

Protection, nutrition, or transportation:
Which service is offered in each situation?
Are there *multiple* benefits, in combination?
Such remarkable give-and-take partners!

All life on our planet is interconnected,
in networks complex, and at times unexpected.
Jump in, turn the page, meet the pairs we've selected—
come meet Earth's remarkable partners!

Two or more species of living organisms can form relationships that last moments, part of a life cycle, or entire lifetimes. Partners that spend most or all of their lives together are **symbiotic** (sym = together; biotic = living).

When a relationship helps everyone in it, it is called a **mutualism**. Mutualists trade helpful services such as nutrition, protection, and transportation. Sometimes one partner enjoys a big benefit (or two) while the other is helped less, or not at all, by the relationship.

If one partner in the relationship is neither helped nor harmed, that partner is called a **commensal**. But an organism that lives closely with another while causing it harm is a **parasite**.

Please Play with the Poems!*

Meet our poetry partners, Daisy and Honey Bee.
They'll show you how they perform poems for two voices ... OUT LOUD!
They use fun critter voices. They create costumes and props together.
Daisy and Honey Bee are remarkable partners in poetry ... *and* in nature.

*For more about poems for two voices, visit page 47.

Hi!

I'm Daisy.   I'm Honey Bee.

We read poems for two voices

OUT LOUD!

I say one critter's lines

and I say the other critter's lines.

If both critters have the same line

(reading straight across, left to right),

we say that line together!   *we say that line together!*

Want to see how we help each other

with poems *and* in nature?

Come along with us—
let's play!

Come along with us—
let's play!

Fringed Ornamental Tarantula

This tree hole crevice,
long and deep,
is where I lurk.
I hunt. I creep.

While I,
with my eight hairy legs
and fearsome fangs,
will let you stay.
I'll scare your predators away.
(Your skin tastes icky, anyway.)

No offense . . .

& Pug-Snout Frog

In this same crevice,
moist and deep,
I tuck in, safe.
I hunt. I keep
those ants from munching
your fine eggs.

None taken!

Large spiders such as tarantulas are perfectly capable of turning frogs into liquid dinner. But the fringed ornamental tarantula and Nagao's pug-snout frog in Sri Lanka often share the same forest tree hole home. The huge spider's predatory presence sends other potential frog eaters—such as geckos and mantids—searching for safer hunting grounds. Meanwhile, the small tree-dwelling amphibian makes meals of marauding ants that might happily munch tarantula eggs.

When the frog's own jellied eggs hatch, its tiny tadpoles *plink-plunk* into the tree hole's rainwater pool, where they benefit from bits of meals dropped by their eight-legged, messy-eater protector.

Isopods   &   Red Seaweed

we kick kick kick
flitting clump to clump
within our tide pool
hiding
in a red seaweed maze

                     within our tide pool

we nibble crusts of algae
from waving red fronds

                     we're a red seaweed maze

tiny pollen-like cells
stick to our bodies and legs

                     you clean our fronds

then the cells drop off
when we shelter and graze

                     you pick up our sperm cells

                     like bees of the sea
                     you pollinate

in the next red clump

                     our ripe, waiting eggs

Along the rocky coasts of Europe and North America, swarms of inch-long isopod crustaceans hide from predators within clumps of red seaweed. These isopods (iso = same; pod = foot) nibble tiny algae growing on the surface of the seaweed's branching fronds. Since those pesky algae can block the solar energy that powers the seaweed's food production (photosynthesis), the seaweed benefits from the Baltic isopods' cleaning.

Scientists recently discovered that as the isopods forage for algae, they transfer sticky, pollen-like sperm cells from male red seaweed clumps to eggs in female clumps. Bees, birds, and other animals have been pollinating flowers as they forage for food among land plants for 140 million years. Marine isopods (or their early ancestors) may have been helping fertilize red algae in the sea for nearly *600 million years*!

Lichen

Crusty, branched, leaf-like,
I'm lichen. A mashup
of fungus plus algae.
From parts: one new whole.

Two or more species
in lifelong togetherness—
that's symbiosis—
and that's how I roll!

The partnership between one fungus species and at least one green alga and/or blue-green alga species creates a brand-new combo organism: a lichen. Lichens are found in nearly all habitats, from frozen tundra to parched desert. They grow on soil, rock, bark, rusted metal, and even on weevils' backs!

In lichen, the fungus partner pulls minerals and water from its growing surface and from the air, and provides structure for its partner algae. The algae living in lichen use their partner's moisture and minerals during photosynthesis to make sugars, which they then share with their fungus "house."

The relationship between two or more different species living together for most of their life cycle is called *symbiosis*.

Mountain Treeshrew   &   Pitcher Plant

I scurry hurry hunt
for a sticky fruit treat,
in a cloud forest where
there are few sweets to eat.

> *Yoo-hoo, mountain treeshrew . . .*
> My pitcher's open lid
> oozes nectar for you.
> Have a lick of my sugary goodness.
> Have *two*!
>
> Your perch puts your bottom
> in perfect position,
> to deposit a nugget of
> pitcher nutrition.
>
> So . . .
> while you sit on the rim
> of my open-air loo,
> relax . . . take your time . . .
> and feel free to poo.

Don't mind if I **doo!**

In the cloud forests of Borneo where fruits and insects are scarce, a small mammal called the mountain treeshrew licks calorie-packed nectar from the inner surface of a pitcher plant's open lid. To reach the sweet nectar, the treeshrew must perch on the pitcher's rim with its hind end hanging over the bowl. As the mammal slowly laps up a meal, its nitrogen-rich treeshrew poo plops into the plant "toilet"! Pitcher plants grow where soils lack nitrogen, a nutrient all plants need to photosynthesize and grow. Most pitcher plants get nitrogen from the live insects they attract, trap, drown, then digest. This mountain treeshrew supplies nitrogen to its Low's pitcher plant partner, then lives to poo another day!

Carrion Beetle   &   Mites

The sweet scent of corpse
fills the air.
I FLY!

                                          We'll climb aboard
                                          and hold tight—
                                          free ride!

Touchdown on fleshy decay
                    is delectable.
Sharing with carrion flies?
                    DETESTABLE!

My eggs hatch in this rot
for my grubs' good nutrition.
But when fly maggots hatch,
they're my grubs' competition.

I *must* eat more maggots!
I *must* eat fly eggs!

                                          We couldn't have walked here
                                          on mini mite legs,
                                          but we'll eat those maggots
                                          and fly eggs, too!
                                          Our flight on your beetlecopter
                                          helped *us* help *you.*

Your mite-y appetites
help my grubs survive!
Yum . . . I smell a new corpse . . .
ALL ABOARD!

                                          LET'S RIDE!

Worldwide, many species of carrion beetles take to the air to follow the scent of newly dead vertebrate animals. These beetles lay their eggs in rotting flesh (carrion), and their young larvae (beetle grubs) hatch surrounded in a deliciously dead food source. But flesh flies and blow flies get to corpses first, laying lots of their own eggs. Their hatching larvae (maggots) compete with carrion beetle grubs for food.

Luckily for these beetles, some species of mites (tiny cousins of spiders) climb aboard for an airlift to far-off carrion, a food source they wouldn't be able to reach on their own eight legs. These hitchhiker mites join carrion beetles in eating pesky fly eggs and maggots, which leaves more mushy rotten food for the growing beetle grubs.

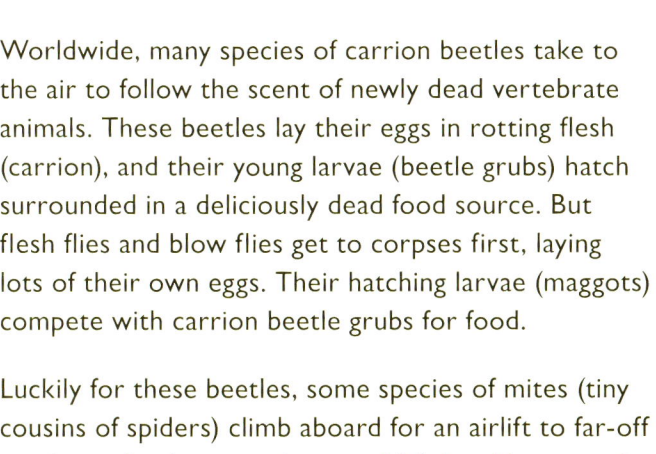

RODENT XING

Ocean Sunfish   &   Laysan Albatross

My skin is a paradise for parasites.
I'm creeping with crawlies and covered in bites.
I swim to the surface and flop on my side,
a fin-tastic dinner plate eight feet wide!

Yo-ho-ho, what's this I see?
A platter of goodies beckoning me!

Cheers to you, Albatross, your wings span the sky.
You glide toward the sea, splashing down nearby.
Now jab your sharp beak at the base of my fin,
plucking bloodsucker pests that get under my skin!

Yo-ho-ho, those suckers were sweet!
SNAPS* for the open ocean treat!

This poem is based on an old sea shanty called "The Eddystone Light."

Scan here and sing along!

* "Snaps" (snapping fingers) is one quiet way listeners show appreciation during a poetry performance.

The odd-shaped, jellyfish-gulping ocean sunfish is the largest bony fish in the world. Known as a deep diver, the sunfish also basks on the surface of tropical and temperate waters, flat side up. Its wide swath of scaly skin makes a convenient feeding station for more than fifty species of troublesome ocean parasites. Hungry seabirds approach when they spot this sunbathing fish displaying such tasty treats. The sunfish lets its avian cleaners dig out pests with their beaks. These ready snacks are a welcome find for an albatross wandering above the wide-open sea.

Many species of cleaner fish and shrimp pick harmful parasites from the skin and gills of larger ocean animals. On land, many cleaner birds enjoy pesty pickings from the pelts of host mammals. But some sly cleaners in both habitats cheat, sneaking harmful nibbles or pecks of their host's protective mucous, flesh, or blood!

Egg-Loving Algae & Spotted Salamander Egg

Inside the egg capsule
we surround
the salamander egg we love
with the green swarm
of our
solar-powered,
oxygen-making,
single-celled
selves.

Inside my egg capsule
that's enveloped in jelly
I divide
I develop
from a single egg cell
into a many-celled embryo,
floating in algae-filled fluid,
enjoying extra oxygen,
expelling carbon dioxide and wastes

that *we* use to flourish
and multiply

while *I* grow
and GROW.

Oophila (which means "egg-loving") are single-celled algae. They live inside the capsules of spotted salamander eggs in eastern North America. Nestled together within a thick jelly envelope, the salamander egg capsules protect the Oophila from being eaten by other animals. Like all green algae, Oophila make food using energy from sunlight plus carbon dioxide (photosynthesis). Oophila get a helpful boost for photosynthesis from the nitrogen wastes produced by the growing salamander embryo.

The extra oxygen the algae give off in the egg capsule during photosynthesis helps the salamander embryo grow strong. But Oophila soon slip inside the growing salamander embryo's body where the sun's energy can't shine. The algae can't make food. This puts them under stress; many die. When the salamander hatches from its egg capsule as a free-swimming larva, its body still contains bits of DNA from its algae partners. Are both partners still benefitting? Scientists are continuing to study this complicated relationship between Oophila algae and their spotted salamander hosts.

Leafcutter Ants & Fungi

Ants farm,

        fungi grow,

in our garden, down below.   in our garden, down below.

Ants forage.
Ants chop.
Leaf bits feed the fungus crop.   Leaf bits feed the fungus crop.

Ants march.
Ants protect.
Ants weed (and poo!) to disinfect.

Ants munch fungi,

        fungi grow,
        safe and cared for
        down below.

Leafcutter ants are the busiest farmers in the tropical Americas and Caribbean. Long lines of leafcutters chop and carry large leaf bits back to their underground colony to feed their food-crop partners, the fungi. Each leafcutter species grows and tends a certain species of fungus that can't live on its own.

One colony can house millions of ants divided into groups called castes, each with a special job. The queen lays eggs. Babysitters care for the newly hatched, worm-like ant larvae. Soldier ants guard the colony while foragers cut leaves and bring them back to feed the underground fungus crop. Gardeners deposit poop droplets that protect their fungus gardens from harmful pests. Garbage haulers remove rot. Leafcutter ants also have bacterial partners on their bodies that help keep the fungi healthy.

Leafcutter ant colonies have been growing their own food instead of hunting, gathering, and scavenging for 8–12 million years, while their well-protected and well-fed fungus partners continue to thrive.

Alligator & Long-Legged Wading Bird

Bird, dear,
when you nest near,
your predators steer clear
of my jaws and sharp-toothed sneer,
while you and *most* of your brood need not fear.
But ... that extra chick you can't rear
and need to disappear?
I volunteer!
I'm here!

Gator, dear,
when I nest near
your jaws and sharp-toothed sneer,
opossums and raccoons steer clear,
while my growing chicks and I need not fear.
Any extra chicks I cannot rear,
they just—*poof!*—disappear.
On we go! We're
still here!

In southeastern wetlands from North Carolina to Texas, long-legged wading birds such as ibises, storks, spoonbills, and herons (like this snowy egret) build their nests on tree islands, above the territories of lurking alligator neighbors. The threat of toothy reptiles below the nests keeps hunting raccoons and opossums away from easy meals of eggs and chicks.

Wading birds typically hatch a couple more chicks than they can feed and raise. Chicks that are weak, dead, or simply "extra" end up in the swamp. The alligators downstairs snap them right up. This extra nutrition helps female alligators lay more eggs, which is important since the survival rate for hatchling alligators is low. Mama gators protect their babies, but the hatchlings feed themselves!

Boxer Crab   &   Anemones

I wrestle for a piece of you,
then quickly rip you into two.
I grip you with my weak front claws
and there you'll grow, as good as new.

                                                                                     Well, *sort of* . . . eventually . . .

Two stinging pom-poms that I swing
when predators are threatening,
you're also good at stunning prey
to snag feasts worthy of a king.

                                                                                     We'd like to feast like kings . . .

Look, I *deserve* the greater share.
Such heavy lifting . . . wear and tear . . .
If you grew huge, who'd ~~catch my food~~ . . . er . . .
                         carry you?
Eat a bit less. *It's only fair!*

                                                                                 But what do *we* get out of it???

Quarter-sized boxer crabs living in the tropical Indo-Pacific Ocean lack crusher claws for attacking prey. Instead, they hook a tiny sea anemone to each delicate front pincer and use the anemones' stinging tentacles to stun and collect prey. Crabs and anemones share the spoils. Boxer crabs also wave or jab their stinger-covered pom-poms at predators for protection. A boxer without anemones will wrestle one from another crab. Then each crab splits its single anemone into two, which both regrow. Does this relationship help anemones? Some scientists think anemones benefit from their crab ride to better-oxygenated waters.

One boxer crab species from the Red Sea limits its anemones' food, keeping themselves well-fed and their anemones tiny. This relationship seems like a bad deal for these anemones, but scientists think they must get some benefit since none have been found living on their own in the wild . . . *yet!*

Hawaiian Bobtail Squid   &   Light-Organ Bacteria

Life is fine in partnership with you!
Illuminated by your blue-green glow,
I match the moonlight, disappear from view.

                                          Life is fine in partnership with you!
                                          We're sheltered, swimming in nutritious brew.

You hide my shape from predators below.

Life is fine in partnership with you,   Life is fine in partnership with you,
illuminated by our blue-green glow!   illuminated by our blue-green glow!

By day, the small Hawaiian bobtail squid hides under sand in shallow island waters. Like all squid, the bobtail can confuse predators with a blob of ink and camouflage its skin to disappear in plain sight. But this small nocturnal hunter has an extra trick up its sleeve—er—mantle!

The bobtail squid has a light organ inside its body filled with light-producing (bioluminescent) bacteria. The squid matches the brightness of moon and starlight above with the amount of blue-green bacterial light it shines downward from its light organ. This trick hides its squiddy outline from monk seals and other predators below. Its disguised outline may even help the bobtail capture prey. The squid's single-celled partners can live free in ocean water, but when these bacteria are bathed in nutritious proteins and sugars inside the squid's light organ, they *thrive*!

Pistol Shrimp   &   Goby Fish

I excavate sand with my feet—
kick–kick–kick so our burrow stays neat.
    Poor vision's no fun.
      A shrimp's work? *Never done!*
Drifting sand washes in: dig, repeat.

                              Your kicks dislodge sand critters—*yum!*
                              And I warn you when predators come.
                                    Did you feel my tail flick?
                                      Let's dart deep inside . . . *QUICK!*
                              Many thanks for our safe burrow, chum!

Tiny pistol shrimp and small fish called gobies are often seen sharing a burrow in shallow tropical and near-tropical seas. The pistol shrimp kicks shifting sands out of its burrow and shores up the entry with bits of shells while the goby stands guard. Poor eyesight makes the shrimp easy pickings for predators. The shrimp works with one antenna touching its fish partner's tail; when the goby flicks its tail in warning, the shrimp darts into the burrow. The goby follows.

The fish benefits from a safe haven *and* from snacks of sand-dwelling critters kicked up by its hardworking shrimp housemate. The shrimp lives to dig another day!

Marsh Frog   &   Water Buffalo

The marsh grows cold and bugs are few
                          in autumn.
We're mobs of frogs, and hungry, too,
                          come autumn.

                                  We buffalo have reeds to chew
                                                    in autumn.
                                When marsh flies bite, we wallow *(whew!)*
                                                    in autumn.

Say . . .
Your fly-filled fur could see us through.
We'll hop up bareback *(WHEE! YAHOO!)*,
a moving feast with full-marsh view.

                                 Guess we'll trade pests for clean-up crew
                                                    in autumn.

Common marsh frogs have been seen foraging for flies in the shaggy fur of Anatolian water buffalos, farm animals that graze on wetland plants in the marshes of northern Turkey. Scientists have observed this surprising relationship in autumn only, when frogs are numerous and their food sources—such as insects—are scarce.

These hungry amphibians benefit from the plentiful fly buffet found in the fur of their wallowing wetland water taxi. Frogs' bodies are heated and cooled by their surroundings—they're **ectothermic**—so as fall temperatures drop, buffalo fur might also provide needed warmth.

Are water buffalos healthier when they host these pest-zapping stowaways? Scientific observations lead to excellent questions . . . *and* further study!

Feathered Dinosaur   &   Beetle Larvae

We shed feathers,
in our nests.
Dino feathers,
what a mess!
Unless . . .

    Unless . . .
    we moved in,
    commenced to chew.
    A cast-off feather
    cleanup crew!
    We ate and ate,
    we grew and grew,
    then trapped in amber,
    left our clue:
    a little pile
    of fossil poo!

A hundred million
years ago,

    A hundred million
    years ago,
    your cast-off feathers
    helped us grow.

Did clean nests
help us dinos?
So . . .
they didn't *hurt*—
that much, we know!

larva in amber

Paleontologists studying remains more than 100 million years old that were trapped in amber (the fossilized resin from ancient trees) uncovered evidence of a special relationship between a feathered dinosaur (theropod) and the grub of a beetle. Preserved in the amber, the grubs' outer coverings (exoskeletons) showed these were early relatives of carpet beetles—beetles with mouthparts built to chew on dried animal parts like feathers. Partly chewed feathers trapped in the same amber had fungi growing on them—a sign of decay. This suggests that the feathers were shed by the dino *before* the beetle grubs chewed them.

The amber sample revealed two additional, important clues: fossilized grub *poop*, and grub exoskeletons of different sizes. These two pieces of evidence show that the ancient beetle grubs digested their feather food and grew!

Did feathered dinosaurs benefit from their nest-cleaning grubs? Some living birds benefit from their insect partners' cleaning services, but clues found in the amber so far indicated only that these dinosaurs were not harmed.

Human Being & Gut Bacteria

Within my gut anatomy—
my colon, more specifically—
bacteria (by the *trillions!*) live
in ecosystem harmony.

    We colonize your colon (yes, it's
    also called your large intestine),
    fill its niches, block invaders,
    and assist with food digestion!

    We train immune cells so they'll know
    which microbe is your friend, or foe,
    and from your gut, we cue those cells:
    Knock out those harmful microbes! GO!

I show my deep appreciation:
food and shelter on location.
Still . . .
sometimes some of you must go,
by process of elimination!

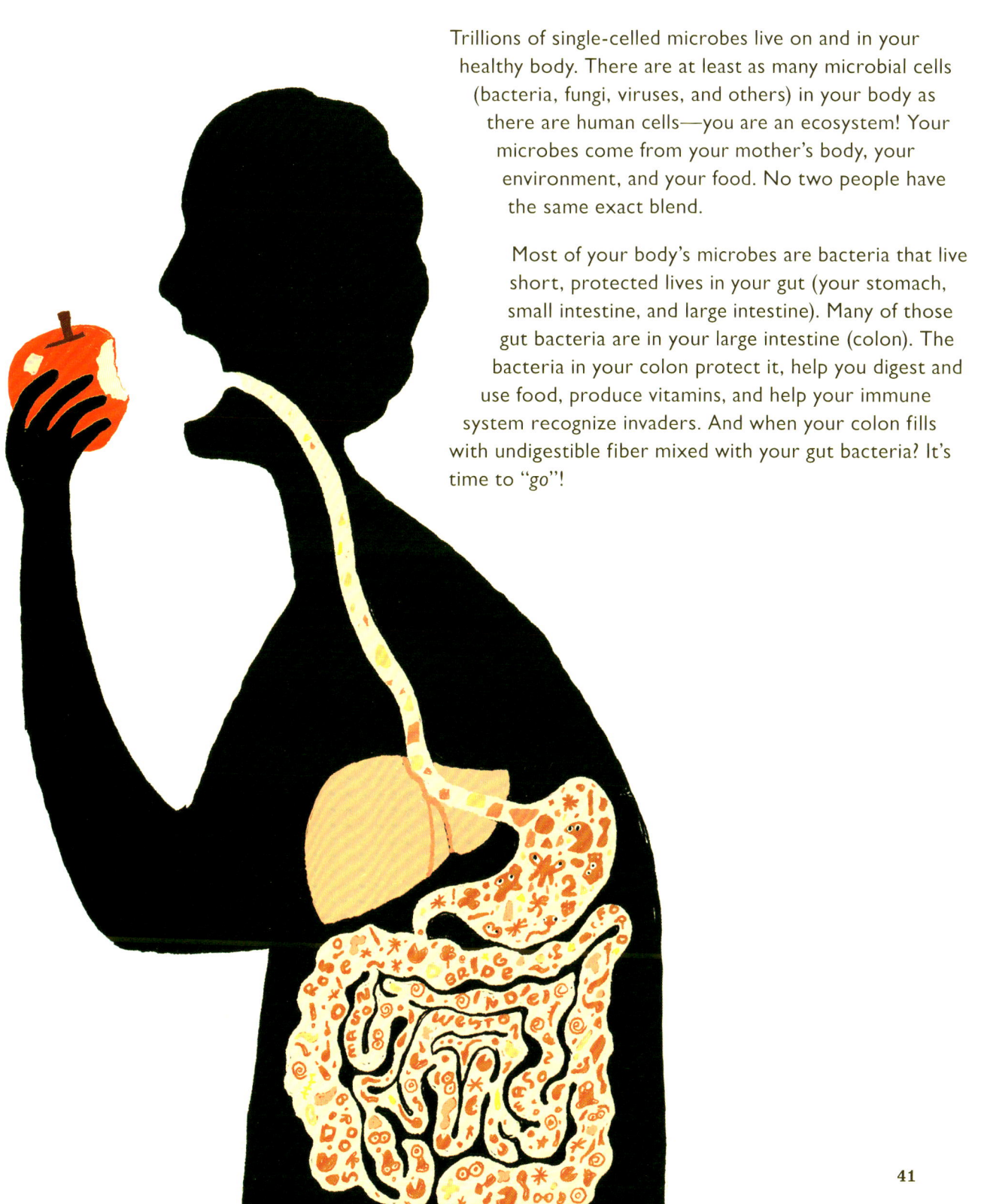

Trillions of single-celled microbes live on and in your healthy body. There are at least as many microbial cells (bacteria, fungi, viruses, and others) in your body as there are human cells—you are an ecosystem! Your microbes come from your mother's body, your environment, and your food. No two people have the same exact blend.

Most of your body's microbes are bacteria that live short, protected lives in your gut (your stomach, small intestine, and large intestine). Many of those gut bacteria are in your large intestine (colon). The bacteria in your colon protect it, help you digest and use food, produce vitamins, and help your immune system recognize invaders. And when your colon fills with undigestible fiber mixed with your gut bacteria? It's time to "go"!

Ecosystem Earth!

Luppity, duppity,
Earth's living species
exist in a richly mixed,
marvelous stew.

Driving Earth's heartbeat of
biodiversity?
Sure, species richness,
but partnerships, too!

Organisms in an ecosystem depend on each other in a network of complex partnerships. These interactions among species are critically important to an ecosystem, helping the system function and maintaining the diversity of its inhabitants.

Loss of species through climate change, ocean acidification, habitat loss, and other human activities can disrupt partnerships and cause extinctions among other species in an ecosystem's network. Let's study, learn, and act to lessen our human impact so we can improve the health of our beautiful and fascinating planet Earth now, and for future generations.

Glossary

alga—a plant or plant-like organism without roots that lives in salt water or fresh water and uses energy from the sun to make food (two or more are called algae)

anatomy—the science of the structure and function of an organism and its parts

avian—related to birds

bacterium—a single-celled organism that is neither plant nor animal and can live independently in soil or water, or live on or inside an animal or plant (two or more are called bacteria)

biodiversity—the different species of animals and plants that live in one area and their interactions

carrion—the dead or decomposing flesh of an animal

cloud forest—a lush, moist, misty rainforest found at a higher elevation

colony—a group of organisms of the same species that live together

corpse—the body of a dead animal

crustaceans—a group of invertebrates closely related to insects but with more pairs of legs, some of which are modified for functions other than walking; most common crustaceans—such as shrimp and crabs—live in water

decay—the breakdown (rot) of organic matter through natural processes of fungi, bacteria, or other organisms

digestion—the process of breaking food down into substances small enough to be absorbed and used by the body

ecosystem—a community of organisms and their interactions with one another and the nonliving parts of their environment

embryo—an early stage of a developing organism

excavate—to dig a hole by removing material

frond—a long leaf or leaf-like structure

fungus—a single-celled or multicellular organism that is neither plant nor animal nor bacterium and feeds on live or dead organic matter; includes mushrooms, toadstools, molds, and yeasts (two or more are called fungi)

gecko—a small lizard with sticky foot pads

grub—the wormy, caterpillar-like young form of a beetle; slang for food

immune cells—the cells produced in bone marrow that fight infection

invertebrate—an animal without an internal backbone

isopod—a small crustacean living on land, or in fresh water or seawater, with seven identical pairs of legs

larva—a newly hatched or immature (young) invertebrate that can look quite different from its adult form (two or more are called larvae)

light organ—a specialized part of an animal's body that contains light-producing bacteria or chemicals that react to give off light

maggot—the worm-like, legless larva of a fly

mammal—a furred or hairy vertebrate animal that makes internal heat to maintain a constant body temperature and produces milk to nourish its infants

mantid—one of a group of large insects that capture and crush their insect prey with their spined front legs

mantle—the sheath covering the internal organs of a squid

microbe—a living organism too small to be seen without a microscope

mineral—a naturally occurring inorganic element or chemical compound; the element phosphorus is a mineral, as is the compound salt (sodium chloride)

mite—a tiny eight-legged arachnid related to ticks

nectar—a sugary liquid that is produced by plants

nitrogen—an element forming compounds needed by all living cells; a component of proteins and DNA

paleontologist—a scientist who studies the evolutionary history of early life on Earth

pollen—the tiny, microscopic grains produced in the male part of a flower or plant that can fertilize the egg in the female part of that plant species to make fruit or seeds

pollinate—to transfer pollen grains to the female part of a plant where the egg waits to be fertilized so it can make fruit or seeds

predator—an animal that kills and then eats other animals

reed—the tall, slender leaf of a marsh plant

scavenge—to find and eat the flesh of a dead animal or plant

sperm—a cell produced in the male sex organs of an animal or plant that joins with an egg cell to fertilize it

temperate—related to Earth's regions between the polar (colder) regions and the tropical (hotter) regions; temperate regions are characterized by moderate and variable temperatures

theropoda—a group of "beast-footed" dinosaurs that included small, non-flying feathered dinosaurs that eventually evolved into today's birds, as well as the largest carnivores such as *T. rex*

tide pool—an isolated pool of seawater that remains after the tide goes out (ebbs)

tropical—related to the region on Earth closest to the equator that is characterized by hot and humid weather

vertebrate—a member of the large group of animals that typically have an internal skeleton with a backbone

Remarkable Partners Species List

Fringed ornamental tarantula *(Poecilotheria ornata)**
Pug-snout frog *(Uperodon nagaoi)*

Baltic isopod *(Idotea balthica)*
Red seaweed *(Gracilaria gracilis)*

Lichen (at least 20,000 species worldwide)

Mountain treeshrew *(Tupaia montana)*
Low's pitcher plant *(Nepenthes lowii)*

Carrion beetle (Silphidae family)
Phoretic (attached for travel) mite *(Poecilochirus spp.**)*

Ocean sunfish *(Mola mola)*
Laysan Albatross *(Phoebastria immutabilis)*

Egg-loving alga *(Oophila amblystomatis)*
Spotted salamander *(Ambystoma maculatum)*

Leafcutter ant *(Attine spp.)*
Ant-farmed fungi (hundreds of species in the class Basidiomycota)

American alligator *(Alligator mississippiensis)*
Snowy egret *(Egretta thula)*

Boxer crab *(Lybia spp.)*
Sea anemone *(Alicia spp.)*
Boxer crab that limits its sea anemone partner's food *(Lybia leptochelis)*

Hawaiian bobtail squid *(Euprymna scolopes)*
Bobtail squid's light organ bacteria *(Vibrio fischeri)*

Pistol shrimp *(Alpheus spp.)*
Goby *(Amblyeleotris spp.)*

Marsh frog *(Pelophylax ridibundus)*
Water buffalo *(Bubalus bubalis)*

Feathered dinosaur (a theropod)
Beetles associated with feathered dinosaurs (many different species in family Dermestidae)

Humans *(Homo sapiens)*
Human gut bacteria (many different species, most classified within two large taxonomic groups [phyla] of bacteria)

*Scientific names are written in the form: (Genus, species).

**The abbreviation "spp." written after a genus name indicates two or more species within a genus group.

More About Poems for Two Voices

Line 1: Ants farm, *(leafcutter ants speak)*

Line 2: fungi grow, *(fungi speak)*

Line 3: in our garden, down below.   *(together now!)*   in our garden, down below.

The format of a poem written for two voices gives information about who is "speaking" each line, and in what order lines should be read. Typically, the lines that belong to one voice are printed in a column on the left and the lines belonging to the other voice appear on the right. For extra clarity, the poet (and/or the book designer) may also assign a different font or font color to each speaker in the poem.

All poems—and *especially* poems for two voices—are meant to be read **aloud**! Each voice speaks on its own line, reading left to right, then down to its next line, or down and across to the other voice's line.

When one voice is speaking the other is silent . . . *unless* both voices are speaking at the same time! Sometimes both voices are speaking together in the poems in this book. These words appear on both the left and the right across the same line. In other books when the same exact words are spoken together, those lines may appear in a middle column.

Poems for two voices offer creative, collaborative FUN for readers *and* writers.

Poetry Notes

Meet the Mutualists! is a poem written in five *stanzas*, or sets of lines. The first three lines *end rhyme* with one another and have four STRONG beats. Each stanza's invitational fourth line has just three strong beats and is a *refrain*—a line or part of a line that is repeated.

Fringed Ornamental Tarantula & Pug-Snout Frog has an end rhyme on every fourth strong beat. Some lines are short, two-beat lines. A few lines are longer. The last two lines don't rhyme with anything and are just for fun!

Isopods & Red Seaweed uses repetition and sometimes both voices speak the same entire line together. This *free verse* (non-rhyming) poem can be read two ways: reading left to right across the columns, moving downward, or reading all of the Isopod column first and then the Seaweed. Does this change the experience and/or meaning?

Lichen is loosely based on the poetic form called the *double dactyl*. One dactyl is a set of three *syllables* (parts of words) we say in the *rhythm* STRONG/soft/soft. Here's a double dactyl: TWO/or/more SPE/cies/in.

Mountain Treeshrew & Pitcher Plant uses end rhyme and rhythm, with extra lines that encourage readers to pause and to have fun!

Carrion Beetle & Mites is a conversation with rhythm and rhyme that connect voice to voice.

Ocean Sunfish & Laysan Albatross is written using the rhythm and rhyme pattern of the old English folk song "The Eddystone Light." Each verse (stanza) is composed of two rhyming *couplets,* or pairs of lines. The two chorus sections are rhyming couplets with a different rhythm.

Egg-Loving Algae & Spotted Salamander Egg is a free verse poem that uses *alliteration* (words next to or near one another that start with the same sound) and *internal rhyme* to give the poem its music. One internal rhyme—a rhyme found within the lines of the poem—is de*velop* and en*velop*ed.

Leafcutter Ants & Fungi uses short, rhyming lines to mimic leafcutter ants on the march across the rainforest floor.

Alligator & Long-Legged Wading Bird has two stanzas each written in a nine-line poetic form called a *rubliw*, which was invented by American poet Richard Wilbur. All nine lines have the same end rhyme. The first line has one strong beat. Each following line adds one strong beat until line five (five strong beats). From line six onward, each line decreases by one strong beat and ends with one strong beat in line nine.

Boxer Crab & Anemones uses the rhyme pattern of a *ruba'i* poem, an ancient Persian stanza form with four lines. Persian is the official language of Iran. In a ruba'i, the first, second, and fourth lines rhyme with one another.

Hawaiian Bobtail Squid & Light-Organ Bacteria is written in the eight-line poetry form called a *triolet*. A triolet has just two rhyme sounds, with a rhyme scheme of ABaAabAB. This poetry notation is like a code with one letter standing for each line. Lines given the same letter (such as A and a) rhyme with each other. Lines represented with the same capital letter (A and A) are exact repeats.

Pistol Shrimp & Goby Fish has two stanzas each written in the form of a *limerick*. The limerick has five lines, two rhyme sounds, and a rollicking rhythm. The first, second, and fifth lines rhyme with one another and have three strong beats in each line. The third and fourth lines have two strong beats and rhyme with each other.

Marsh Frog & Water Buffalo is inspired by an ancient Middle Eastern poem form called a *ghazal*. As in a traditional ghazal, this poem is written in rhyming couplets, and both lines in each couplet also end with a repeated word or phrase—I used "in autumn." The end stanza of the poem does not follow the rhyme scheme of a traditional ghazal form.

Feathered Dinosaur & Beetle Larvae is a rhyming poem with no regular pattern in a form I like to call *free rhyme*.

Human Being & Gut Bacteria is another poem inspired by the aaba rhyme pattern of the four-line ancient Persian poetic form, the ruba'i.

Ecosystem Earth! is a traditional double dactyl. The first line contains two nonsense words in the STRONG/soft/soft dactyl rhythm. The second line is the "name" of the subject of the poem. All lines have two STRONG/soft/soft dactyls except the fourth line in each stanza, which has the rhythm: STRONG/soft/soft/STRONG. The second line in the second stanza is one long word made of two dactyls: BI/o/di/VER/si/ty.

Nature's Wild Relationships

Surprising Combinations*

While exploring which critters might fit my circus performer theme for *Amphibian Acrobats*, I came across an article about tiny marsh frogs that hopped aboard water buffalos in Turkey. *Bareback-rider frogs?* I thought. *Perfect!* I'd seen fish nibbling pests from sharks while scuba diving, and I read on to see if this was a similar mutualistic cleaner-host relationship. The answer was "maybe." *Relationships in nature are complex and fascinating!* I said to myself. So instead of casting these marsh frogs in my amphibian circus, I tucked the frog and buffalo pals in a new "Unlikely Partners" idea file. Since many readers might already be familiar with charismatic companions such as clownfish and anemones, I kept my eye out for other combinations of critters that surprised me or added to my understanding of familiar partners.

Is It Symbiosis or Mutualism?

I began this project reading widely on the topic and learned that definitions for the terms **mutualism** and **symbiosis** have evolved over time, and conventional understandings differ.

Mutualism is a relationship that benefits both partners. In **commensalism**, one partner benefits and the other is neither helped nor harmed. When one partner benefits and another is harmed, that's **parasitism**.

In current scientific usage, **symbiosis** is a close relationship between partners that persists over time. A symbiotic relationship can be mutually beneficial, neutral, or harmful. If a mutualistic, commensal, or parasitic relationship is not close and long-term, it is not considered symbiotic.

*This book highlights and celebrates two-critter partnerships. In nature, ecological communities are complex webs of partnerships that enhance the survival and reproduction of organisms and help their ecosystems function.

Wild Examples!

A cleaner shrimp that helps rid fish of parasites and scores a meal for itself is mutualistic! Win-win! But the cleaner shrimp may have many clients, and its client fish may have many cleaners. *Not* symbiotic!

Sub-Saharan oxpeckers are also cleaners who get juicy tick meals in exchange for ridding herbivores of skin parasites. Mutualists, right? But these birds may also widen wounds to help themselves to their hosts' blood—so they may be mutualists who are sometimes parasitic!

Even in clearly mutualistic relationships, providing benefits can cost a partner energy (a pitcher plant uses energy to make nectar to attract a mountain treeshrew, for example). These costs and benefits among partners may not be equal. In addition to field observation, the scientific understanding of mutualistic relationships requires rigorous investigation. We know that the marsh frogs mentioned in "Surprising Combinations" find ready insect meals in buffalo fur. We may assume Turkish water buffalos benefit from hosting fewer pests. But further study is needed to quantify whether buffalos with amphibian passengers are indeed healthier. There's always more to learn about ecosystem Earth!

Symbiosis and Mutualism: A Bibliography

Bronstein, Judith L. ed., *Mutualism.* Oxford University Press, 2015. A study of mutualism and its rewards and benefits, including different forms of mutualism and many examples in nature. The author defines *symbiosis* as the persistent relationship between two organisms whether mutually beneficial, commensal, or parasitic. A *symbiotic mutualism* is a mutualism with persistent and prolonged physical intimacy between the participants, as opposed to mutualistic relationships that do not persist for all or most of an organism's lifespan.

Douglas, Angela E. *The Symbiotic Habit.* Princeton University Press, 2010. This volume defines *symbiosis* as a persistent relationship with the requirement that all participants benefit, with the caveat that the benefit can be costly to provide.

Gilbert, Scott F. "Symbiosis as the way of eukaryotic life: The dependent co-origination of the body." *J. Biosci* 39 (2014): 201–209. https://doi.org/10.1007/s12038-013-9343-6. Recent scientific developments indicate that organisms—plants, microbes, *and* animals—are composites of larger organisms living and evolving with numerous smaller ones.

National Geographic Society. "Symbiosis: The Art of Living Together." Accessed 8 February 2025. https://education.nationalgeographic.org/resource/symbiosis-art-living-together. A succinct, leveled, explanatory biology/ecology article for grades 3–12 with definitions and examples using the definition of *symbiosis* that relies on persistence, not mutual benefit.

Acknowledgments

I am continually surprised and delighted by the generous, thoughtful communications I receive from scientists in the field. Their enthusiasm deepens my understanding and helps my writing reflect the excitement and nuances of their scientific inquiries. My poems celebrate the fascinating work of these remarkable science partners:

Dr. Thasun Amarasinghe (fringed ornamental tarantula and pug-snout frog), Dr. Jeff Ollerton and Dr. Zong-Xin Ren (marine isopods and red seaweed), Dr. Walter Fertig (lichen), Dr. Chris Thorogood (mountain treeshrew and pitcher plant), Dr. Cole Gilbert (carrion beetle and mites, leafcutter ants and fungi), Dr. Hiroji Onishi (ocean sunfish and Laysan albatross), Dr. John Burns (egg-loving algae and spotted salamander egg), Dr. Lucas A. Nell (alligator and long-legged wading birds), Dr. Yair Achituv (boxer crab and anemone), Dr. Margaret McFall-Ngai (Hawaiian bobtail squid and light-organ bacteria), Dr. Piotr Tryjanowski (marsh frog and water buffalo), Dr. Ricardo Pérez-de la Fuente (feathered dinosaur and beetle larvae), Dr. Cathryn Nagler (human being and gut bacteria).

Special thanks to my diver friend John Belgrove for his keen interest in this topic and his delight in the pistol shrimp and goby mutualism.

Love and gratitude to Julia Hirsch for her arrangement and performance of "Ocean Sunfish & Laysan Albatross." Thanks to Robert Meganck for his remarkable critters.

Endless thanks to Margaret Quinlin and all the Peaches for years upon years of every kind of support. I am deeply grateful to my editor, Vicky Holifield, for her kindness, care, and enthusiasm throughout our long and remarkable bookmaking partnership.

Margaret Quinlin Books
An imprint of Peachtree Publishing Company Inc.

Text copyright © 2026 by Leslie Bulion
Illustrations copyright © 2026 by Robert Meganck

All rights reserved. No part of this book may be reproduced, transmitted, or stored in an information retrieval system in any form or by any means, graphic, electronic, or mechanical, including photocopying, taping, and recording, without prior written permission from the publisher. Additionally, no part of this book may be used or reproduced in any manner for the purpose of training artificial intelligence technologies or systems, nor for text and data mining.

Printed and bound in November 2025 at C&C Offset, Shenzhen, China.
The illustrations were rendered digitally.
Edited by Vicky Holifield
Illustration and design by Robert Meganck
Art direction and composition by Lucy Ricketts
PeachtreeBooks.com

First Edition
10 9 8 7 6 5 4 3 2 1
ISBN: 978-1-68263-780-7 (hardcover)

Library of Congress Cataloging-in-Publication Data

Names: Bulion, Leslie, 1958– author | Meganck, Robert illustrator
Title: Nature's remarkable partners : wild poems for two voices / written by Leslie Bulion ; illustrated by Robert Meganck.
Description: First edition. | Atlanta, Georgia : Margaret Quinlin Books, 2026. | Includes bibliographical references. | Audience: Ages 8–12 years | Audience: Grades 4–6 | Summary: "These wild poems for two voices offer young readers an up-to-date peek at an intriguing array of symbiotic partnerships in nature. Most upper-elementary students are familiar with mutually beneficial partnerships in nature--butterflies and milkweed, for example, or clownfish and anemones. But award-winning science poetry author Leslie Bulion has delved into recent research on mutualism and found fresh examples of these relationships for young readers to investigate, including the egg-laying carrion beetle and its hitchhiking mite passengers, as well as the little goby fish that guards the pistol shrimp from predators in exchange for a safe haven. Reading aloud these clever verses for two voices will help young learners engage with and enjoy these marvels of nature, and notes in the back of the book shed more light on the diversity of poetic forms. In addition, brief science notes accompanying each featured partnership, and comprehensive back matter provides more opportunities for study. Robert Meganck's witty drawings add another layer of fun to this humorous gallery of perfect partners. This collection is ideal for cross-curricular learning, including units on biology, mutualism, and poetry. Other popular science poetry collections by this creative team are Superlative Birds, Amphibian Acrobats, and Spi-ku, a book about the trick-filled world of spiders"— Provided by publisher.
Identifiers: LCCN 2025028398 | ISBN 9781682637807 hardcover
Subjects: LCSH: Nature—Juvenile poetry | Mutualism (Biology)—Juvenile poetry | LCGFT: Nature poetry
Classification: LCC PS3602.U386 N38 2026 | DDC 811/.6—dc23/eng/20250617
LC record available at https://lccn.loc.gov/2025028398

EU Authorized Representative: HackettFlynn Ltd, 36 Cloch Choirneal, Balrothery, Co. Dublin, K32 C942, Ireland.
EU@walkerpublishinggroup.com